REAL REVOLUTIONARIES

THE REAL
GEORGE
WASHINGTON

THE TRUTH BEHIND THE LEGEND

by Eric Braun

COMPASS POINT BOOKS
a capstone imprint

Real Revolutionaries is published by Compass Point Books,
1710 Roe Crest Drive, North Mankato, Minnesota 56003
www.mycapstone.com

Library of Congress Cataloging-in-Publication Data is on file with the Library of Congress.
Names: Braun, Eric, 1971– author.
Title: The real George Washington : the truth behind the legend / by Eric Braun.
Description: North Mankato, Minnesota : Compass Point Books, [2019] |Series: CPB grades 4-8.
Real revolutionaries | Audience: Ages 10-14.
Identifiers: LCCN 2018042075| ISBN 9780756558901 (hardcover) |
ISBN 9780756561260 (pbk.) | ISBN 9780756558956 (ebook pdf)
Subjects: LCSH: Washington, George, 1732-1799—Juvenile literature. |
   Presidents—United States—Biography—Juvenile literature.
Classification: LCC E312.66 .B68 2019 | DDC 973.4/1092 [B] —dc23
LC record available at https://lccn.loc.gov/2018042075

Editorial Credits
Nick Healy, editor; Sarah Bennett, designer; Eric Gohl, media researcher; Kathy McColley,
production specialist

Photo Credits
Alamy: Glasshouse Images, 20, Maurice Savage, 51, North Wind Picture Archives, 13, World
History Archive, cover, 1; Getty Images: Culture Club, 26, Kean Collection, 33, Photo 12, 56–57,
Stringer/Archive Photos, 24; Library of Congress: 9, 11, 31, 38, 44; New York Public Library: 7,
17, 28–29, 43, 53; Newscom: Everett Collection, 37; Wikimedia: Metropolitan Museum of Art,
40–41, US Capitol, 48–49

Design Elements
Shutterstock

Contents

CHAPTER ONE

A MONUMENTAL LEADER

George Washington did so much to help establish the United States of America, he is known as the "father of our country." He risked his life, served in many roles, sacrificed again and again, and led with honor. Even his political enemies admired him. It's difficult to boil down a list of his most important accomplishments, but it would have to begin with his military command.

COMMANDER OF THE FIRST CONTINENTAL ARMY

A fist fight in Boston started because troops from Massachusetts teased soldiers from Virginia. They said the Virginia soldiers had silly uniforms. They even threw snowballs at the southerners. The Virginians yelled back. Soon, a huge fight broke out. That's when General George Washington showed up.

Washington had come to
Boston to take the job of leading
the newly created Continental
Army. When the general
saw his own men fighting
one another, his heart
must have sunk. The
challenge the American
colonists faced was hard
enough. The British had

many advantages. And now more than 1,000 of his own
men were brawling. How could they expect to defeat the
enemy if they couldn't even get along together?

But if Washington lost any hope at that moment, he
did not show it. Instead, he rode his horse right into the
middle of the fight. All around him, men were punching,
kicking, wrestling, and shouting. He leaped from his
saddle and grabbed two of the tallest, strongest men by
the neck. He shook them. When the other men saw their
angry general, they scattered. They didn't fight again.
Washington had broken up the fight before it led to
serious consequences for both sides.

This moment was an example of Washington's
strength and leadership. It showed the respect his men
had for him. He was exactly the leader that the rebels
needed. But he never wanted the job.

In the summer of 1775, George Washington was
a wealthy landowner. He was a planter and part-time

legislator in the American colony of Virginia. Twenty years earlier, he had been a leader in the French and Indian War (1754–1763). He fought for the British against the French in the unsettled lands west of Virginia. He gained a name for himself as a leader with great courage and honor. Then, in 1759, he married the wealthy widow Martha Custis. He left the military. He and Martha settled into life together at his estate at Mount Vernon. Over the next decades, he bought nearly 8,000 acres (3237 hectares) of prime farmland. He farmed tobacco and other crops.

But Washington and other colonial farmers and businessmen were frustrated. They resented the taxes and other forms of British interference. They formed a Continental Congress to address their issues with Britain. Washington joined as a Virginia delegate.

Tensions with the British were growing. By the late 1760s, British and colonial troops in Massachusetts were fighting over taxes and other issues. In 1775, the Continental Congress decided to create a Continental Army. The goal was to gather troops from across the colonies. Members of the Congress selected Washington to lead the brand new army.

The appointment was a great honor for Washington. But he felt unprepared. His last military service had been nearly 20 years earlier. In a letter to his wife, Washington described his feelings about his new responsibilities. It "fills me with inexpressible concern," he wrote. Rather than seeking out the job, he had "used every endeavor in

Washington took command of the Continental Army in 1775. He faced a difficult task in fighting well-trained British forces.

my power to avoid it." But, he added, refusing to take the challenge would have "reflected dishonor upon myself."

So in early July 1775, Washington arrived in Boston. He was ready to lead the newly created Continental Army. It was a nearly impossible task. The British troops were highly trained. They had money from Britain. The Continental Army was made up of soldiers from the 13 colonies, which had joined to declare their independence. Most were part-time soldiers. Very few had any serious or prolonged training. Many had poor-quality weapons. Some had none.

The Continental Army had another problem. The soldiers were not united. They felt loyal to their own colonies but not to the larger Continental Army. That was what led the Massachusetts and Virginia soldiers to fight each other. Ultimately, Washington was able to unite the militias in their common cause.

WASHINGTON'S STUNNING VICTORIES

Washington's goal as commander of the Continental Army was to drive the British from the colonies. But his army was short on money, supplies, and trained soldiers. To make things worse, Washington's troops faced one of the world's mightiest militaries. The British Army and Navy were world powers.

But from the beginning, Washington showed that he could outsmart his enemies. His first goal was to force British troops out of the city of Boston. The British had occupied it since they won the Battle of Bunker Hill early in the war. Washington knew his untrained troops couldn't drive the British out of Boston. But he lined up heavy artillery outside the city and bombarded it for two days. Then he ordered the guns moved to a higher position in Dorchester Heights, which also overlooked the harbor where the British had ships. The British knew they could not withstand bombardment from those guns at that elevated position. They retreated from Boston on March 17, 1776.

Later, the Continental Army suffered several stinging defeats. Five months after they retreated from Boston, British forces defeated Washington's army in the Battle of Long Island in New York. In the following months, the British drove the revolutionary troops south through New Jersey. In the middle of December, Washington retreated with his army south across the Delaware River. They camped on the Pennsylvania side of the river. The winter was bitterly cold. They had very little food, ammunition, or supplies.

Washington and Marquis de Lafayette oversaw troops during a difficult winter at the Valley Forge encampment. A lack of food and supplies there left men vulnerable to life-threatening illnesses.

Washington knew he needed to act to turn the tide. He planned a surprise attack on the British forces across the river in Trenton, New Jersey. (Actually, the soldiers in Trenton were Hessians, or Germans, who were fighting for the British.) He would cross the river with his 2,400 men. Two of his generals would meet him at Trenton with another 2,600 soldiers. Washington expected to succeed behind the might of 5,000 men.

On Christmas Day, he crossed the icy river with his troops. Then they marched 19 miles (31 kilometers) through an ice storm to reach Trenton. Right away a problem arose for Washington. The other two generals and their men hadn't reached Trenton. Washington and his soldiers had to face a larger army on their own.

But the Hessians at Trenton were not prepared for Washington's surprise attack. Washington fired cannons on the enemy camp. He split up his troops and had them attack from two sides. The Hessian commander was shot and killed. Before long the Hessians surrendered. In the end, Washington's troops killed 22 enemies. They also wounded 92, and captured 918 Hessians. Washington lost only two soldiers. (They both froze to death.)

Little more than a week later, he led his men to an even larger surprise victory at the Battle of Princeton in New Jersey. British General Charles Cornwallis had been advancing on Washington with a huge army. Washington convinced men from local militias to join the Continental Army for the big battle. To trick Cornwallis,

In January 1777, an American victory at the Battle of Princeton became an important turning point in the war.

Washington left campfires burning in camp while he and about 5,000 men sneaked away under cover of night. When Cornwallis attacked the camp in the morning, he found it nearly abandoned. Meanwhile, Washington and his men were fighting at Princeton. Washington himself rode through gunfire, leading by example. Soon the Continentals won Princeton, taking many prisoners and supplies. Washington had established himself as a first-rate commander.

The Revolutionary War (1775–1783) went on for six more years. Washington's army had more successes and more setbacks. One of his biggest victories was the 1781 Battle of Yorktown. In that battle Washington was joined by the French Navy. The combined forces attacked the

British stronghold at Yorktown. The battle lasted three weeks. When the British surrendered, everyone knew the Revolutionary War was over. George Washington received much of the credit for winning the war and gaining independence for a new nation.

A UNANIMOUS CHOICE FOR PRESIDENT

The Revolutionary War ended in 1783 when Great Britain signed the Treaty of Paris. George Washington had earned the admiration and respect of his people. But his job leading the Continental Army was complete. And he was eager to return to private life. He moved back to his Virginia farm, Mount Vernon.

For the next few years, Washington kept busy at Mount Vernon. He was glad to retire from public life. He enjoyed taking over day-to-day business on his farm and vast estate. And he enjoyed spending time with his wife, Martha.

But the new country needed a stable government. Leaders from all the states gathered in Philadelphia in the spring of 1787. Their goal was to write a constitution. Before that, the country was governed by the Articles of Confederation and Perpetual Union. But it had become clear that the Articles were not sufficient to address all the problems of the new country. They did not give the federal government the power to tax, which it needed to raise money. And it did not have ways for resolving disputes between states. So the new document would better describe how the states would work together as one united country. The gathering was called the Constitutional Convention. Delegates from each state attended. They represented the people of their states.

Washington did not want to join the convention. For one thing, he liked being home on his farm. For another, he didn't want people to think he was trying to seize power in the new country. But the delegates wanted Washington to join them. They knew that citizens throughout the former colonies trusted George Washington more than anyone else. He was the new nation's first hero.

Washington agreed to attend the Constitutional Convention. The delegates elected him president of the convention. But he tried to let others make the decisions. One decision was whether the new country's top leadership post should be filled by one person or a small group of equal leaders. Also at issue was how much power the states should have and how much power the central government should have. None of the delegates wanted any one person to have the power of a king.

The delegates worked through the hot Philadelphia summer. By September they had a first draft of a constitution for the United States. It described how the new government would have three branches that share power. There would be one president, a congress with the power to tax, and a national court system.

Now the writers had to convince leaders from each state to approve the document. Another convention was held in Richmond, Virginia, in 1788. On June 25, that convention voted to approve the Constitution. Finally it was time to elect the nation's first president.

The Constitution said exactly how the vote for president should proceed. A total of 69 electors representing each of the states would vote. The votes would be sealed and delivered to the Senate, where they would be counted. Washington had made it clear he did not want to be president. He went home to Mount Vernon, his estate in northern Virginia, while the voting took place.

Meanwhile, winter weather caused a delay, and the votes were not counted until several weeks later than had been planned. When they were, nobody was surprised: George Washington received all 69 votes. In 1789, the nation's first president was elected unanimously.

Washington felt his duty to his country was greater than his duty to his personal wishes. The United States needed a strong leader the people could trust. So he accepted the presidency.

The young country celebrated the election with fireworks. People flooded the streets of New York, where the inauguration was held. (New York was the nation's capital at the time.) Ships flew flags and fired guns and cannons. Bells rang out. The crowd of happy people was so thick, one person said he thought he could walk on top of people's heads. Washington gave a speech. When finally it was time for him to go home, his carriage could not get through the party in the streets. Instead of riding, the new president had to walk to his New York residence.

George Washington took the oath of office to begin his presidency at Federal Hall on Wall Street in New York City.

CREATING A FEDERAL GOVERNMENT

Being president meant Washington was the head of the executive branch of the government. His job was to work with the two other branches of government to lead the country. The other two branches were the legislative (Congress) and the judicial (courts). Together, the three branches needed to create and maintain all the systems and laws to guide the new nation.

The U.S. Constitution set the rules for the new government. It defined the rights of U.S. citizens. And it described what the government is and is not allowed to do. It also explained what the federal government would be responsible for and what would be left to the state governments.

But Washington and others soon realized the Constitution did not have answers for all the issues the new country would face. For instance, one big problem was that the states had huge debts. They had borrowed money from France and other countries to pay for the Revolutionary War. The new government had to decide how to repay those debts. Should each state pay its own debt? Or should the federal government pay for the cost of the war?

The Constitution did not say anything about how to repay debts. Leaders in the new government argued about what to do. Some wanted to create a national bank. This bank could establish one national currency. It could pay the war debts. But others argued that this was too much power for the central government. In the end, Congress voted to open a central bank. Washington signed the bill into law in 1791.

Policies for money and debt were only a part of what Washington would establish for the United States. He also had to decide how the country would interact with other countries. Would the United States get involved in other countries' wars, as France and Germany had been involved in the American Revolution?

The French Revolution started in 1789—the same year Washington became president. French rebel leaders asked Washington for support. He believed in the cause of the French Revolution, in which France's people rose up against their king and queen. But he also believed that the United States should not get involved. The country was too young and in too much debt. He believed the country should stay neutral. He issued the Proclamation of Neutrality. It stated that the United States would stay out of the war in France. It set the direction for the United States, which would stay out of other countries' affairs for more than a century to come.

Washington also established the president's cabinet. This is a group of advisors. Each one is the head of a different department. Washington's cabinet had four people. Thomas Jefferson was the Secretary of State. Alexander Hamilton was the Secretary of the Treasury. The Secretary of War was Henry Knox. Edmund Randolph was the attorney general. The cabinet has been an important part of the presidency ever since, but it has many more members in modern times. Today the president's cabinet has 15 members.

Washington regularly conferred with his cabinet. It included the secretaries of state, treasury, and war, along with the attorney general.

MAKING HISTORY BY STEPPING ASIDE

George Washington made history in many important
ways. He joined the colonial leaders who declared their
independence from Britain. He led the Continental
Army to win the Revolutionary War. He became the first
president of the United States and led the new nation
wisely for eight years. But some historians say the most
important thing he did was to step down from being
president.

Washington served two four-year terms as president.
Then he chose not to run for re-election. Today, the
United States has a law saying a president cannot serve
more than two terms. But in Washington's time, there
was no such law. There was nothing to stop Washington
from holding power longer.

But Washington had larger goals in mind. He believed
strongly in the values of the United States. He thought
that a government should exist to protect citizens' rights
to life, liberty, and property as stated in the Declaration
of Independence. And he believed that it should be up
to the citizens to decide who should lead the government.
He did not believe that anybody should be king for
life—or at all. That was what he had fought against in
the Revolutionary War.

Before he was even elected president, Washington
had been clear about not holding power too long. After
the Treaty of Paris ended the Revolutionary War, he
resigned his position as commander of the Continental

Army. Many people were surprised. It was common for a war hero to hang onto power after a victory. Often such military leaders made themselves ruler for life.

Washington's decision to resign his command surprised even his enemies. The news reached King George III of England. He famously asked his American painter, Benjamin West, what Washington planned to do next. He couldn't believe he would give up power. West told him he had heard that Washington would return to his farm. The king replied, "If he does that, he will be the greatest man in the world."

So it should not have been a great surprise when Washington said he would not run for re-election in 1796. But it was. After all, he was popular. If he had decided to run again, he would most likely have won again. One reason he did not run was that he was eager to return to private life. He wanted to live out his old age on his farm with his wife. But another reason was that he wanted to set a precedent. He wanted to be an example for future presidents. And he was. It became an unwritten law that presidents should only serve two terms. No president ran for a third term until Franklin Roosevelt in 1940. But Roosevelt was the first and only president to serve more than two terms. Congress passed the 22nd Amendment in 1947. It states that a person can only be elected to be president two times. It seems that the American people decided that Washington had been right.

CHAPTER TWO

WASHINGTON IN TALL TALES

George Washington is the subject of many legends—some true and some more fiction than fact. Some of the most well-known tales about him are actually myths, though they do demonstrate traits about the first president that are real and important.

"I CANNOT TELL A LIE"

One of the things almost everyone knows about George Washington is his strong sense of honesty. It turns out, however, that one of the best-known stories about his honesty is, well, a lie.

The story goes like this: When George was 6 years old, he was given an ax as a gift. He loved his ax and set to work chopping wood on his family's land. But he accidentally chopped down a valuable cherry tree. His

Many artists have created paintings showing the scene of young George Washington chopping his father's cherry tree.

father was angry when he found out. He demanded to know what had happened. George was afraid he would be in trouble if he told the truth. But he was more afraid of being dishonest. So he looked at his father and said, "I cannot tell a lie." He admitted to chopping down the tree. His father was so proud that his son had told the truth, he stopped being angry. He said that George's honesty was worth more than a thousand trees.

For two centuries, people have used that cherry tree story to describe Washington's honesty. After all, it's a great story. Not only that, it helps people believe that Washington was a great leader not just because of what he did, but because of who he was—on the inside. The story shows that Washington had a good and honest character. Americans have found it feels good to believe that one of the founding fathers was so honest.

Most historians agree that Washington was probably very honest. But they also agree that the cherry tree story is a myth. It simply never happened.

The myth was most likely invented by Mason Weems. Weems was a writer who published *The Life of Washington* in 1800. The book was an instant best seller. It told many stories of George Washington's great virtues. But it did not include the cherry tree story when it was first published. That story first appeared in the book's fifth edition, which was published in 1806.

The myth spread when another writer picked up on it. William Holmes McGuffey included the cherry tree story in his children's book series called the McGuffey Readers. He also used the story to illustrate the importance of being honest. McGuffey was a teacher and minister who believed strongly in teaching morals to children.

The myth also showed up in an unusual place: It was told by a circus woman named Joice Heth in the 1830s. Heth was an enslaved woman bought by the circus owner P.T. Barnum in 1835. She was made into a sideshow

Mason Weems's *The Life of Washington* included stories and illustrations that created legends about the life of Washington.

attraction. Barnum claimed she was the slave who had raised George Washington. Circus customers paid money to hear Heth tell stories of young George. Since she didn't actually know Washington, she told the stories that were printed in Weems's book.

It's not clear when it became common knowledge that the cherry tree story is a myth. Modern historians agree it was a tall tale. Yet people today still use the story to illustrate the virtue of honesty.

TOSSING A COIN ACROSS A RIVER

A famous legend about George Washington is that he was so big and strong he could throw a silver dollar across the Potomac River. But is that true?

It's true that he was big. At nearly 6 feet, 3 inches (191 centimeters) tall, he was one of the taller men in colonial America. Some histories claim that Ben Franklin once said, "We always choose him to lead us because he was always the tallest man in the room." In other accounts it was John Adams who noted that Washington's height gave him authority. Whatever the case, it is clear that Washington's height commanded attention.

It's also true that Washington was strong. He was known as a sportsman. He was good at most of the popular sports of his time, such as archery, swimming, and wrestling. His favorite sport was horseback riding. He was an excellent rider, and he had the powerful muscles to do it well. He rode for pleasure around his vast farm. And he spent much of his time in the military on horseback. He also loved hunting. He rode horses as part of that sport as well.

Clearly, Washington was tall and strong. But did he actually throw a silver dollar across the Potomac River? It's unlikely. For one thing, silver dollars didn't even exist until 1794. Washington would have been 62 years old by then. But even setting aside nitpicking about what type of coin was involved, this tale remains very unlikely. Coins were worth a lot of money—and Washington was known for being thrifty with money. Most historians agree that he would not have thrown any away.

Some versions of this legend say that it was a rock, not a coin, that Washington threw across the Potomac. But even this story is unlikely. Flowing past Washington's home at Mount Vernon and the site of the nation's capital at Washington, D.C., the Potomac River is a major body of water. It's so wide, it would be impossible for anyone to throw an object across.

There is one version that might be closer to the truth. In his book *The Life of Washington*, Mason Weems tells a more believable story. He says that as a boy, Washington and his friends used to throw rocks into the Rappahannock River. And, he writes, Washington was so strong that he once threw his rock clear across—about 300 feet (91 meters). That's about a football field's length from end zone to end zone. While throwing a rock that far would be an amazing feat, it wouldn't be impossible.

Mount Vernon, Washington's estate, sits on the banks of the Potomac River.

There were other stories of Washington's strong throwing arm. One was told by the artist Charles Wilson Peale. He said that during a visit to Mount Vernon, a group of men started a contest. They wanted to see how far they could throw an iron bar across the lawn. When Washington took a turn, Peale was amazed. He said the bar "lost the power of gravitation and whizzed through the air, striking the ground far, very far, beyond our utmost limits." Then, as he walked away, Washington told his guests, "When you beat my pitch, young gentlemen, I'll try again."

WASHINGTON'S WOODEN TEETH

Many people have heard the story that George Washington had wooden teeth. It's repeated in many books, stories, and memes. What do historians know about this myth?

Washington certainly wore false teeth, or dentures. He had dental troubles from a very young age. Proof of that lies in the detailed personal records he kept. When he was 24, he wrote in his diary that he paid five shillings to a "Doctr Watson" to remove one of his teeth. His diaries and letters are full of stories about his terrible teeth. He often described how much his teeth hurt. He also mentions swollen gums and other mouth troubles.

Washington's collection of letters includes many notes to his dentists. In some, he is ordering tooth-cleaning equipment. He ordered many of the tools of the day, such as tooth powder and a tongue scraper. In other letters, he complains about pain. And sometimes he asks for new dentures.

During the Revolutionary War, one of Washington's letters to his dentist fell into enemy hands. In 1781, the British captured a package of letters sent by Washington. One of them was a letter ordering cleaning supplies from his dentist. Some reports say that Washington was embarrassed when he learned the enemy had read this.

But it turned out that the captured dentist letter helped Washington's army. In the letter, he told his dentist that he would probably not make it to Philadelphia

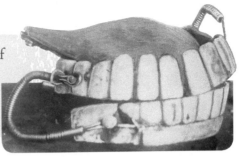

Washington used several sets of false teeth during his lifetime. He eventually lost all of his real teeth.

as planned. He asked the dentist to send his supplies to New York instead. The British thought they had learned a secret. They thought it meant that Washington would be taking his troops to New York. That meant he would not be taking them south, toward Yorktown, Virginia. Partly for that reason, the British did not send extra troops to Yorktown. And partly for that reason, Washington won a huge victory at Yorktown in September 1781. That battle ended up deciding who won the war.

But Washington's poor teeth were not a secret in the colonies. One of his fellow military officers said that Washington's "mouth is largely and generally firmly closed, but which from time to time discloses some defective teeth." Washington himself was embarrassed by the poor state of his real teeth. And, he once wrote, his false teeth "bulge my lips out in such a manner as to make them appear considerably swelled."

But were those false teeth made of wood? Historians say no. They were probably made of many different things. Some were made of human teeth. Others might have been cow or horse teeth. Metal was also used. When they got very stained, they probably looked like wood. That might be where the myth comes from.

MILITARY MISTAKES

George Washington is often remembered as a great military leader. After all, he led the Continental Army to victory over the powerful British Army. One of the most famous stories—and images—of the Revolutionary War is of Washington crossing the Delaware River. The brave midnight crossing of the icy river led to a surprise attack against the British.

One reason Washington was asked to lead the Continental Army was his reputation as a young military star. He had led dangerous battles in the French and Indian War, in which the British and French were fighting over land. Washington was a major in the Virginia militia and was chosen by the British to lead expeditions and negotiate with the French.

But was he a hero? Not exactly. It turns out that Washington's earliest military work was less than perfect.

In the spring of 1754, Washington led a group of soldiers on a dangerous mission in western Virginia. At that time, the area was wilderness. Washington's mission was to stop the French from taking over lands claimed by the British. For nearly two months, Washington led his troops on a difficult journey through thick wilderness. It was so challenging that some days they only traveled 1 mile (1.6 km). Along the way, they had help from the Six Nations Iroquois warriors. This tribe was native to the area. They were caught in the middle of the French and British quests for land. But they usually sided with the British.

George Washington was a young officer in the Virginia militia when he battled a larger French force. He was forced to surrender to them on July 3, 1754.

The Iroquois leader, called Half-King, gave information about the French to Washington. Together, Washington and Half-King decided to launch a surprise attack on the French. They sneaked up on French troops at dawn one morning. The battle lasted about 15 minutes. Washington's men killed 10 French soldiers, including the French commander. They also took two prisoners.

Washington was delighted by his victory. He wrote a letter bragging about how easy it had been. "I heard bullets whistle," he wrote. "And believe me, there is something charming in the sound."

There was one problem. Even though France and England were struggling over the same land, they were not at war. Until then, the two nations had officially been at peace. In fact, the French he had attacked were not even soldiers. They had been on an exploring mission. Now the French wanted revenge. Washington had started the French and Indian War.

Things got worse. Washington soon heard that French troops were coming to attack him. His friend Half-King warned him to build a strong fort for his troops. But Washington didn't listen. Half-King began to think Washington was foolish. Just two weeks later, the French troops were getting close to Washington's position. Now his men tried to quickly build a fort. But Washington and his soldiers did a poor job. The French attacked, and Washington lost 30 soldiers. Another 70 were wounded. With little chance of victory, he surrendered to the French.

After the surrender, Washington made another mistake. The French sent him a letter of surrender to sign. One part of the letter said that Washington admitted to "assassinating" the French commander in the earlier battle. But the letter was in French. Washington did not get a good translation. He did not understand that he was admitting to assassinating a French commander. So he signed the letter. And the French held the "assassination" against the British for the rest of the war.

CHAPTER THREE

THE UNKNOWN WASHINGTON

While Washington's greatest achievements are well-documented, he led a long and varied life full of many accomplishments. From the time he was a young boy, he sought knowledge and adventure.

A SKILLED SURVEYOR

Before Washington was a soldier or officer, and well before he was a politician, he was a surveyor. His job involved measuring land and establishing official boundaries. Surveyors today are skilled workers, but in Washington's time they performed the job without modern tools and technology. It was challenging and exacting work.

Washington learned his skills at school as a young teenager. He practiced these skills on the land at Ferry

Farm, the Virginia farm where he grew up. He was good at math. He was also patient and detail oriented. These skills helped him succeed as a surveyor—as they would help him later in the military and in politics. He also loved the outdoors. He liked horse riding, hunting, fencing, and swimming in the river.

When his father died, young George used the surveying equipment he left behind. He practiced his skills around the farm. One of the first pieces of land he surveyed was a 5-acre (2-hectare) area on Ferry Farm called Hell Hole. His drawing of that land is now at the Library of Congress.

In March 1748, he got his first chance to be a part of a survey expedition. A local friend invited Washington to join his group, which was going to measure plots of land on the Virginia frontier. George, just 16 years old, was the only member of the group who had to get permission from his mother to go. She did not want him to leave the farm. She needed his help with chores. But after he told her he would be paid, she agreed.

Washington and the crew spent about a month in the wilderness. They dragged heavy chains and equipment through the wild terrain. They worked in rain, and at times they were low on food. They met local Native Americans and camped with them. George learned a lot and worked hard. When they finally finished, George was quite ready to return home.

A year later, Washington was hired to be the surveyor for the newly formed Culpeper County in western

Washington's work as a surveyor supported the settlement of land in western Virginia and set boundaries for public and private properties.

Virginia. His first job there was to survey a tract of 400 acres (162 hectares).

Washington was only 17, but he had a good job and a promising career available to him. He left his job as official surveyor in 1750, but he kept doing it professionally. By 1752, Washington had surveyed more

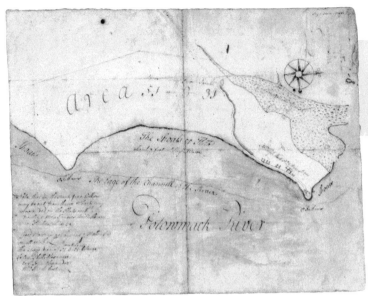

Washington's survey of the site of Belhaven, Virginia, 1748.

than 60,000 acres (24,280 hectares). After that, he still surveyed for personal reasons. He used his skills to figure out his own land boundaries and defend them. He also used surveying to divide, buy, and sell property.

Washington's work as a surveyor influenced the rest of his life. He was known to carry a compass and perform measurements even while serving as president. When he toured the 13 states as president, he recorded land features just as he did when surveying. His study always had plenty of charts and maps.

One of the last survey jobs he did was on November 5, 1799. He surveyed part of his land and some other nearby land that was owned by another man. Washington noted that the man owed him rent and that the man offered a piece of land as payment. Washington died just a few weeks later.

QUELLING A REBELLION

The United States was born from protest and rebellion. Many colonists were unhappy with the way they were treated by Great Britain. They protested against British laws, and paying taxes to the Crown was one of their top complaints. Once they won independence from Great Britain, Americans no longer had to pay British taxes. They had a new government. This government created new laws. And new taxes.

Soon some Americans began to complain about their new government. The first major protest of the United States had to do with taxes. It led to a short but violent rebellion. It was up to President George Washington to end this rebellion.

The problem began in 1791. The young United States was poor. It owed large debts to other countries that had helped it fight the British. Secretary of the Treasury Alexander Hamilton needed to find a way to pay off those debts. He came up with the idea of a tax on whiskey.

A lot of whiskey was made in the United States. Farmers in the western areas of the new country often made whiskey from the crops they grew. One reason they did this was because it was cheaper to ship whiskey back east than it was to ship the crops. These farmers did not like the new tax. They thought it would make them lose money. And they thought it was unfair. They believed the government was asking whiskey makers to pay too big a share of the country's taxes.

Dislike of the whiskey tax was strongest in western Pennsylvania. Farmers and whiskey makers refused to pay the tax. At first they protested peacefully and sought relief from the tax. President Washington stood firm. He said they had to pay. In 1794, the protests turned violent. In July of that year, a mob of about 400 protesters burned down the house of a tax collector in near Pittsburgh.

This violent outburst was the first big challenge to the new U.S. government. The stakes were high. If the rebels succeeded in avoiding the tax, it would set a bad

example for the future. It could undermine the new government and leave it weak and ineffective. Washington knew he needed to act fast. He needed to show that the government was strong.

Sending a few troops would not deliver a strong enough message. Washington ordered nearly 13,000 troops to head to western Pennsylvania. And, to make more of a statement, he personally led the troops to Pittsburgh.

President Washington reviewed troops in a show of force that helped halt the Whiskey Rebellion.

His show of strength worked. By the time the troops reached Pittsburgh, most of the rebels had heard he was coming and gone home. The troops rounded up about 150 rebels. They were charged with treason—a serious crime that means attempting to overthrow the government. In the end, most of the rebels were let go. Two were found guilty. But instead of punishing them, Washington gave them a pardon and let them go home. He had made his point. Washington had successfully ended the first rebellion against the United States.

HIS PARTING ADVICE

In 1792, George Washington's first term as president was coming to an end. He wanted badly to step down. He longed to return to his farm at Mount Vernon. He was tired of the criticism that came with being president. And he was not doing well financially. He even asked his friend James Madison to write an address announcing his retirement.

But for many, the idea of a United States without George Washington as president was scary. People feared that without his leadership, the country would not keep its spirit of unity. People with different political views would fight. The country, which was still so young, might splinter apart. But almost everyone trusted Washington. Even Thomas Jefferson, a political rival, urged him to stay on for a second term.

In the end, Washington agreed. He wanted to make sure the nation was in good shape before he stepped down. So he ran for re-election. And in 1793, he began his second term.

But by the end of his second term in the summer of 1796, Washington felt that things were different. He no longer felt his country needed him. He decided he would not run for re-election.

Before he stepped down, Washington wanted to share his thoughts on his country. He wanted to talk about why he was not running again. And he wanted to outline his ideas for the country's future. He revised some of Madison's address from four years earlier. Then he asked another friend, Alexander Hamilton, to help him finish it. In 1796, Washington edited the final draft. It was 32 pages long.

And although it was written as a speech, Washington did not deliver it in front of an audience. Instead, it was published in a newspaper in the nation's capital, then Philadelphia, in September 1796. Other newspapers quickly picked it up and reprinted it. Soon the news had spread all over the country.

Washington's address came under the headline, "To the PEOPLE of the UNITED STATES." He opened with the words, "Friends and fellow citizens." This showed that he was talking to the citizens, not to government. It was a signal that he believed the power in the country belongs to the people.

In his address, Washington talked about how much he loved his country. Then he talked about the core beliefs that he hoped would continue to guide the United States. He described how important he felt the central (federal) government was. He told Americans to remember they were American first before they were Virginians, New Yorkers, or the like. He said not to let local differences weaken the national unity. He said a strong national government offered more stability than local governments do.

Washington warned about the influence of political parties in his farewell address, which was printed and read throughout the country.

Washington explained what he saw as two big dangers to the United Sates. The first, he said, was political parties. He said that political parties could weaken the strength of the country. But an even bigger danger, he said, were foreign entanglements. He warned Americans to stay out of other countries' business. He called for the United States to remain neutral when other countries were at war with each other. He said all countries need to look out for their own interests first.

Washington's farewell address became known as his most important speech. In fact, for nearly 100 years, it was considered the most important address in American history. Other leaders referred to it often. And in the 1860s, members of Congress began reading it aloud to mark Washington's birthday each year. Today, the U.S. Senate still selects a senator to read the address each year.

CHAPTER FOUR

AN IMPERFECT PRESIDENT

*H*istory often remembers people as either heroes or villains. But most people, including George Washington, are more complicated. Though Washington had many great qualities, some darker truths are a part of his story.

A LACK OF EDUCATION

There is no doubt that George Washington was admired by his peers. He was selected to lead the Continental Army in the Revolutionary War. And he was elected president twice. He also owned one of the most impressive estates in Virginia.

But in one way, Washington always felt he wasn't good enough. He did not have the education that his peers did. Thomas Jefferson, John Adams, and James Madison all graduated from college. Washington never even went to college.

Washington's father was a wealthy planter in Virginia. He had two sons and a daughter with his first wife. After she died, he married Mary Bell. George was the first of their six children together. Unfortunately, George's father died when George was only 11 years old. In his will, he left most of his land to George's older half brothers. George's mother received barely enough money to take care of George and his five siblings.

George's older half brothers had gone to school in England. This was common for the sons of wealthy families. But after his father died, there wasn't money for George to do the same. He could only attend a local school near his home. He worked hard and did well at math. He also read whatever books he could find. But he never studied Greek or Latin or some of the other subjects that his wealthy peers did. When he was 15, he stopped going to school. Instead of going to college, he got his job as a surveyor.

For the rest of his life, Washington tried to make up for not going to college. One of the most important things he wanted to learn was how to behave in polite company. He studied an old etiquette manual. It was called *Rules of Civility and Decent Behavior in Company and Conversation*. It included rules for showing respect to others and for being polite and proper. One rule was, "Cleanse not your teeth with the table cloth, napkin, fork, or knife."

Washington also watched closely how educated gentlemen behaved. He practiced what they did. And he made sure he always behaved as they did in public.

Still, he felt inferior. He had not been to Europe, as they had. And he did not know French, Greek, or Latin, as they did. Behind his back, other colonial leaders made comments about his lack of education. John Adams once said Washington was "too unlearned [and] unread for his

Although Washington worried about his lack of education, he won the admiration of the others who took part in the Continental Congress.

station and reputation." Even when he was a powerful and popular president, he still worried what people thought of him.

Later in life, Washington often spoke of the value of education. He encouraged his nieces and nephews to pay attention in school and do well. He once warned a young relative who was about to go to college to study hard. "Every hour misspent is lost forever," he said.

WASHINGTON AND SLAVERY

In 1796, George Washington was serving his last year as
U.S. president. He learned that an enslaved person in his
household had run away to New England. He wrote to a
friend asking for help getting the slave back. In the letter,
Washington said that he might be in favor of freeing
enslaved people. However, he said, his slaves were still
his property. He wrote that it would not be right to let
one slave go. It would be unfair to his other slaves who
remained with him. He would be rewarding a runaway
with freedom.

This story shows Washington's strange logic and
mixed feelings about the practice of slavery. He knew that
enslaved people (or their ancestors) had been kidnapped
from their homes in Africa and taken to America. They
had been sold as property to white people and forced to
work hard for no pay. At some point in his life, he seemed
to understand that this was simply wrong. It surely did
not reflect the idea that all people are created equal.

Washington had become a slave owner at the age of
11 and owned slaves for most of his life. Most wealthy
Virginia farmers of his time did. Slave labor kept the
farms running and kept profits coming. Slaveholders such
as Washington gave the enslaved people basic necessities
such as food, housing, and clothes. But they controlled all
parts of the slaves' lives. Many owners treated their slaves
cruelly, and all slaveholders considered the slaves to be
property. They bought, traded, and sold them. Few white

Slave quarters at Mount Vernon, as they appear for today's tourists

people talked of slavery as evil. Washington struggled with the question of slavery. He sometimes wrote and spoke of his desire to end it.

When Washington was presiding over the Constitutional Convention, helping to create the new government, the lawmakers discussed—and disagreed about—slavery. Many wanted to make sure the practice would not be a part of the new country. But Southern lawmakers felt strongly that slavery was critical for the country to survive and thrive. They insisted that it stay. Washington did not join the push for the end to slavery. He decided it was too risky. If states fought over it, he feared, not all the states would agree to be a part of the government. In the end, the practice of slavery was allowed to continue.

By the time Washington became president of the United States, his opposition to slavery was growing.

He still had slaves. But he said in private that he wished not to. In a letter to a friend, he wrote that slaves were "property—which I possess, very repugnantly, to my own feelings; but which . . . necessity compels." Still he did not use his power to try to end slavery. He understood that it was an issue that would divide the country bitterly. In the end, he decided that it was more important for the young country to stay together and grow stronger—even if it meant allowing human beings to be enslaved there.

Some stories say that Washington was kinder to his slaves than other owners. But other stories say he was cruel. Whatever the case, we know that Washington thought of his slaves as part of his wealth. He was very worried about how much money they cost him. He kept records of how much he spent on food, clothing, and housing for slaves. And he recorded how much work his slaves did. Some of his slaves worked in the fields growing crops. Others worked in the house sewing clothes and fixing furniture. Washington expected them all to do set amounts of work. He once wrote about checking on his slaves in the dead of winter. He wanted to make sure they were working hard, even though it was very cold.

By the time of George Washington's death in 1799, Mount Vernon had 317 enslaved people living there. Washington left instructions in his will that after Martha died, all the slaves on his property would be freed.

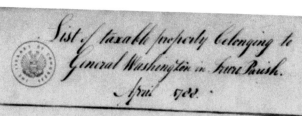

A 1788 list of the Washingtons' taxable property included the names of enslaved people at his Virginia estate.

CHAPTER FIVE
STANDING FOR HONOR

One afternoon in December 1799, George Washington mounted his horse. It was very cold, and at times that day it snowed, hailed, and rained. But over the next five hours, he toured his farms. He checked out the grounds and made plans for projects. He returned home soaking wet and freezing cold, but the next day he went out again in even more snow.

By now he had a sore throat. But there was work to do. He marked trees he wanted to cut down. He planned to build a fishpond near the river. And he was frustrated to note that some of his cattle stalls were dirty.

Over the next few days, Washington's cold got worse. It became hard for him to speak or breathe. His wife, Martha, began to worry. She called for a doctor, who brought in two more doctors. They tried various procedures that were popular then, including bleeding him. They cut into him to let out several pints of blood. But these treatments could not improve his symptoms.

Washington's personal secretary was Tobias Lear. As Washington struggled to breathe, Lear turned him in the bed to make it easier. Washington was a big man, and it was hard work. Washington told Lear that he worried this lifting and turning would fatigue the younger man. It was only one small comment. But it said a lot about who George Washington was. Just as he had for most of his life, he thought more about others than himself—even while he was dying.

George Washington believed strongly in a code of honor. To him, that meant he did what was right. He behaved as a gentleman. He cared for others and for the greater good more than he did himself.

This quality may be the most important aspect of George Washington's legend. He did not want to be the nation's first president. He loved being a farmer and wanted to retire to Mount Vernon. Who could have blamed him if he had? He had already served in two wars for his country. He had won American independence! Hadn't he given enough?

But Washington knew that the nation needed him. There was nobody else the people trusted as much as him. Without a fair and highly respected president, the country might have fractured. People had strong opinions about how to forge the new government. And they were ready to fight over it. So Washington accepted the job. And when he wanted to retire after one term, he instead ran for a second. Again it was what the nation needed.

Just as important, Washington left office after those two terms. Many leaders crave power over everything. They want to remain in charge. But Washington knew that the U.S. president needed to share power. That's what was best for the greater good. When he stepped down so that someone else could have the job, he sent

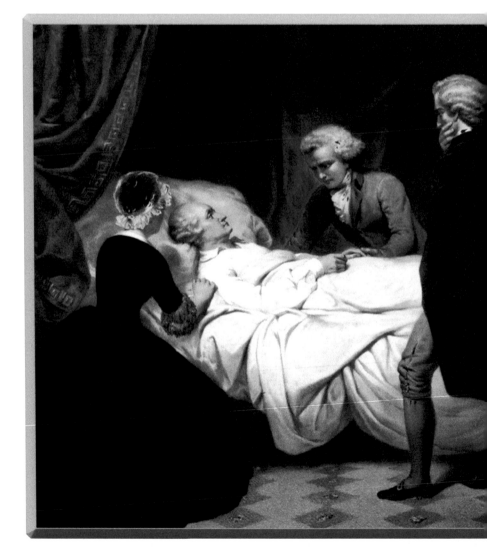

a message not only to American citizens. It was also a message to the rest of the world: *This is what a democracy looks like.*

Washington must have been in great pain while he was dying. His throat was swollen shut. Nearly half of his blood had been drained by doctors who didn't know better. But he never cried, yelled out, or complained. He would not have wanted to worry Martha or anyone else.

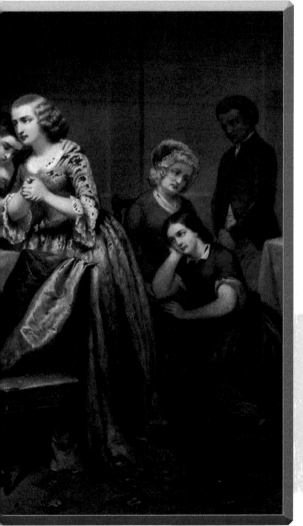

Finally, with his fingers, Washington checked his own pulse on his wrist. In that moment, it stopped. His hand fell to the bed.

George Washington's final hours were painful. An inflamed throat made breathing difficult for him, and doctors' attempts to help actually caused more pain and worsened his condition.

TIMELINE

1732

George Washington is born in Virginia on February 22.

1749

Washington begins his first job as the official surveyor
for Culpeper County, Virginia.

1755

Washington is appointed Colonel of Virginia,
making him commander of all armed forces in the colony.

1759

Washington marries the widow Martha Dandridge Custis.

1769

Washington presents a resolution to the Virginia House
of Burgesses opposing taxation without representation.

1774

Washington is elected delegate to the
First Continental Congress.

1775

In April, the first shots of the Revolutionary War
are fired at Lexington and Concord, Massachusetts.
In June, Washington is appointed general and
commander-in-chief of the new Continental Army.

1776

In July, General Washington and others sign the
Declaration of Independence. In December, Washington
crosses the Delaware River and, by sneak attack,
wins the Battle of Trenton, New Jersey.

1779

The Continental Congress approves a peace plan calling for colonial
independence and for the British to leave the colonies.

1781
The British Army surrenders at Yorktown, Virginia.

1783
The Treaty of Paris is signed by the United States
and Great Britain, ending the Americans'
fight for independence.

1787
Washington is elected president of the
Constitutional Convention in Philadelphia.

1789
Washington is elected first president of the United States.

1793
President Washington is elected to a second term
as president of the United States.

1794
President Washington leads troops to Pennsylvania
to end the Whiskey Rebellion.

1796
President Washington publishes his farewell address
as a public letter. John Adams is elected second president of the
United States (after Washington does not run for re-election).

1797
Washington returns to his estate at Mount Vernon.

1799
On December 14, Washington dies at Mount Vernon
at the age of 67. In his will, he asks for his slaves to be freed.

GLOSSARY

colonist—a person who lives in a state or territory that is under the control of another country

constitution—a document that outlines the basic beliefs and laws of a nation, state, or social group and that establishes the powers and duties of the government and guarantees certain rights to the people in it

Continental Army—the army made up of soldiers from all the colonies who fought Great Britain in the Revolutionary War

executive—of or relating to the carrying out of laws and public and national affairs, as in the executive branch of government

federal—a form of government in which power is distributed between a central authority and individual units, such as states

judicial—of or relating to courts or judges, as in the judicial branch of government

legislative—of or related to making laws, as in the legislative branch of government

militia—a body of citizens with some military training who are usually only called to active duty in an emergency

neutral—not favoring either side in a quarrel, contest, or war

precedent—something that may serve as an example or rule to be followed in the future

rebellion—resistance to authority; armed defiance of a government

repugnant—causing a strong feeling of disgust

unanimous—agreed to by all

virtue—a quality of moral excellence

FURTHER READING

Marciniak, Kristin. *The Revolutionary War: Why They Fought.* Mankato, Minn.: Capstone Press, 2015.

Raum, Elizabeth. *A Revolutionary War Timeline.* Mankato, Minn.: Capstone Press, 2014.

Thompson, Ben. *Guts & Glory: The American Revolution.* New York: Little, Brown and Company, 2017.

INTERNET SITES

Use FactHound to find Internet sites related to this book.

Visit *www.facthound.com*

Just type in **9780756558901** and go.

SOURCE NOTES

p. 8–9, "fills me with…" George Washington. *Washington: A Life*. New York: Penguin Books, 2010, p. 188–189.

p. 22, "If he does that…" King George III. "The Man Who Would Not Be King," by David Boaz for the CATO Institute, Februrary 20, 2006. https://www.cato.org/publications/commentary/man-who-would-not-be-king. Accessed August 24, 2018.

p. 29, "lost the power of gravitation…" Charles Wilson Peale. "First in War, First in Peace, First in Sports?" George Washington's Mount Vernon. https://www.mountvernon.org/george-washington/the-man-the-myth/athleticism/. Accessed August 24, 2018.

p. 29, "When you beat my pitch…" George Washington. "First in War, First in Peace, First in Sports?" George Washington's Mount Vernon. https://www.mountvernon.org/george-washington/the-man-the-myth/athleticism/. Accessed August 24, 2018.

p. 31, "mouth is largely and firmly closed…" Captain George Mercer. "Washington's Tooth Troubles." https://www.mountvernon.org/george-washington/biography/washington-stories/dentures/. Accessed August 24, 2018.

p. 31, "bulge my lips out…" George Washington. "Washington's Tooth Troubles." https://www.mountvernon.org/george-washington/biography/washington-stories/dentures/. Accessed August 24, 2018.

p. 33, "I heard the bullets whistle…" George Washington. *Patriots: The Men Who Started the American Revolution*. New York: Simon and Schuster, 1988.

p. 44, "Friends and fellow citizens…" George Washington. "Transcript of President George Washington's Farewell Address (1796)." https://www.ourdocuments.gov/doc.php?flash=false&doc=15&page=transcript. Accessed August 24, 2018.

p. 48, "too unlearned [and] unread..." John Adams. *Washington: A Life*. New York: Penguin Books, 2010, p. 13.

p. 49, "Every hour misspent is lost forever." George Washington. *Washington: A Life*. New York: Penguin Books, 2010, p. 13.

p. 52, "property–which I possess..." George Washington. "Master and Employer" by Paul Leicester Ford, collected in *George Washington: People Who Made History*, San Diego, CA: Greenhaven Press, 2003.

SELECT BIBLIOGRAPHY

George Washington's Mount Vernon
http://www.mountvernon.org/

Karen Price Hossell, editor. *George Washington: People Who Made History*. Farmington Hills, Mich: Greenhaven Press, 2003.

Ron Chernow. *Washington: A Life*. New York: Penguin Books, 2010.

The Man Who Would Not Be King
https://www.cato.org/publications/commentary/man-who-would-not-be-king

INDEX